, 2000

rk of
ed

be used or reproduc
written permission exce
in reviews. For informat
55 Avenue Road, Suite 290
nada M5R 3L2.

rpercanada.com

g in Publication Data
tle:
dian English Dictionary

668-7
guage - Dictionaries. I. Sutherland, Fraser.
2000   423   C99-932311-3

ntered words that we have reason to believe
constitute trademarks have been designated as
such. However, neither the presence nor
absence of such designation should be regarded
as affecting the legal status of any trademark.

Typeset by Wordcraft, Glasgow

Printed and bound in Great Britain by
Omnia Books Ltd, Glasgow G64

First Published 1902
Previous Editions 1936, 1954, 1963, 1981, 1987, 1991, 1994
Canadian Edition First Published 1987

New Edition 2000
Reprinted 2001

10 9 8 7 6 5 4 3 2

© HarperCollins Publishers
1902, 1936, 1954, 1963, 1981, 1987, 1991, 199

Collins Gem® is a registered tradem
HarperCollins Publishers Limi

All rights reserved. No part of this book ma
in any manner whatsoever without prior
in the case of brief quotations embodie
address HarperCollins Publishers
Toronto, Ontario, C

http://www.h

Canadian Cataloguin
Main entry under t
Collins Gem Can
New ed.
ISBN 0-00-638
1.English la
PE1628.C5

Collin
An Imprint of HarperCollins